Information Security based on ISO 27001 Strategies

A Leadership Introduction to Information Security in
the Service, Education and Manufacturing Industry

Christian Bartsch

1st English Edition 2023

Revision 03/2026

ACATO BOOKS

ACATO BOOKS

USA | UK | EU | Canada | Australia
India | Mexico | Brazil | Japan

ACATO Books is part of ACATO GmbH
whose addresses can be found at acato.de

First published in USA by ACATO Books in 2023
First published in UK by ACATO Books in 2023
First published in ACATO Books in 2023

ISBN: 979-8-8651-4150-1 Paperback (English)
ASIN: B0CNPNGTR6 Kindle Edition (English)

ISBN: 979-8-3213-4257-2 Paperback (German)
ISBN: 979-8-2763-4049-4 Paperback (Spanish)
ISBN: 979-8-2544-6278-1 Paperback (French)

Publisher's DISCLAIMER

Any internet address, phone numbers, or company or product information printed in this book are offered as a resource and are not intended in any way to be or to imply an endorsement by ACATO Books, nor does ACATO Books vouch for the existence, content, or services of these sites, phone numbers, companies, or products beyond the life of this book. All reasonable efforts have been made to correctly attribute the intellectual property of unique concepts of others. Every person referenced in this book has been contacted by the author to have their quotes, concepts or information approved.

Revision-No. 1.04 ENG / 2026-03-31 — 18-18

CONTENTS

1 Introduction

The information technology industry has been one of the key motors of information security management initiatives. Eventually other industries adopted similar approach to information security and cyber security **control and improvement**. This is why it is so important for medium to large businesses to have an ISO 27001 certification even if you do not yet have acquired an ISO 9001 certification. As the world of **services, education & manufacturing** become an even more digital businesses, it is necessary to protect the intellectual property stored in information companies share with their suppliers and partners. This also expands to components that are highly integrated in a digital way. Hence, ISO 27001 eventually became the key information security standard. If you are new to ISO 27001 then you might be aware of **ISO 9001 Standard**, that is related to quality management. The **2022 Release** of the ISO 27001 Standard is now emphasizing the importance of **data privacy and cyber security**.

At this point your mind should start asking these questions:

- Why should my company achieve an ISO27001 Certification?
- When does my company need to start a ISO27001 project?
- How can we generate a sustainable outcome?

Let's face it. It can be quite frustrating to see revenue fall, just because your company did not invest the effort into getting ISO 27001 certified or even reaching any **quality management system (short: QMS) certification**. Let me now show you in an informative and hopefully also useful way how you **get ready for an** ISO27001 audit. If you follow this rapid introduction to information security in your industry, you will experience a better outcome for your company's future.

From personal experience in the services and manufacturing industry, I understand how complex and challenging is doing business for suppliers with large clients. Even the education sector is having to implement a QMS and ISMS based on the global ISO standards. This affects small training facilities providing government sponsored career education, too.

Today I am involved with a variety of service / education / manufacturing industries, since I became involved with a venture investment company. Eventually this allowed me to put my experience to improving **information security** by working on **standard related auditing** (ISO 9001, ISO 27001) projects.

Today, I advise companies on, how to get their ISMS documentation ready for certification. My clients are SMEs, European holdings and technology driven manufacturers. As I am also active on the auditing side, I understand what large certification bodies expect to be a compliant **Information Security Management System** (ISMS). TISAX and ISO 27001 can put substantial pressure on an organisation, if the project becomes bloated. I want you to avoid running into useless courses, overpriced advice and outdated templates that force you to act against your gut feeling.

Yours

Christian Bartsch

PS: If you would like to get advice on how to ..., don't hesitate to contact me at c.bartsch@acato.de.

Do you need more strategical insights before the day?

Get the strategy book: books.meetchrisbartsch.com

Trust me: it is worthwhile the effort to mind feed now!

2 Why ISO 27001 matters in your Industry?

In the following sections I will answer for you following questions:

- Why should I care as an executive?

- How can ISO 27001 be explained to me in short and simple terms?

- Hat impact will it have on my success?

- Where will I feel pain if I ignore ISO 27001?

- What can be done?

As you notice, above questions gradually guide you into understanding the impact of ISO 27001 and how to best tackle ISO 27001 so you do not have to suffer any negative impact. If you do experience unforeseen stress due to ISO 27001 this might be an indicator that you are not taking advantage of its positive opportunities.

2.1 What is ISO 27001?

Let me introduce you to ISO 27001 in a compact and understandable language:

The abbreviation "ISMS" stands for **Information Security Management System**.

ISO 27001 is used by a wide range of industries to reach a standard guiding the management of information security of companies, which might become suppliers or joint venture partners.

Hence, ISO 27001 is an **information security management framework**. By agreeing on ISO 27001 as a common assessment and evaluation framework, the global community has **simplified the recognition of companies making an effort to protect sensitive and personal information**. Thereby, customers, partners, suppliers and authorities have less workload in demonstrating their information security commitment.

Before ISO 27001 every major information handling organisation had very different understandings of how management of information security should be handled. This strained companies who needed very different documentation to satisfy the regulations of each key client or government body.

With introduction of ISO 27001 companies of all industries could focus more on one common standard, which had been designed on the learnings of previous data leaks and scandals.

As information is increasingly becoming a digital inter-connected asset of a company's competitive advantage, **cyber-attacks are a significant operational risk**. Hackers are known to have gained access to the networks of manufacturers, universities, gaming platforms and large telecommunication organisations. Those events hackers accessed consumer data, confidential design, research and operative data.

The digital **theft of trade secrets** is a substantial threat to the western industry sectors. ISO 27001 tries to address these substantial threats and also achieve greater awareness within these organisations.

Companies that are compliant with the requirements of ISO 27001 can **build trust with their customers, partners and suppliers**. Governments are increasingly aware of the cyber risks looming in their vital sectors as authorities, businesses and consumers are increasingly interacting with each over in a digital environment.

Hackers, cyber terrorists and digital warfare can **disrupt society and the economy** of a nation.

2.2   How it can become a competitive advantage

ISO 27001 is used by organizations to **improve their information security, cyber resilience and manage cyber threats** in a more sustainable way. Thereby, organizations become aware of the current cyber risks and the potential existential harm a breach could cause. Not only manufacturing can be disrupted but also unforeseen digital product risks could evolve from attackers intentional manipulation of the manufacturing process.

This commitment to ISO 27001 allows companies to **display their full commitment** to ensuring an acceptable level of information security to protect all stakeholders. Hence, a company with ISO 27001 implementation will be perceived as a trusted business partner.

Large manufacturers implement a just-in-time and lean management strategy. A security breach at a supplier can disrupt the entire supply chain and costs millions per day, as production comes to a painful stand still. A company using ISO 27001 will not be able to prevent every security breach, but it will have done everything one should expect of them to prevent it from causing harm to others.

Hence, ISO 27001 sets **best practices** for managing information security, **facilitating collaboration** and **building trust** between companies of all sorts (e.g., Suppliers, Manufacturers, Designers, Research Institutes, HR Recruiters & Training Facilitators).

Being compliant with ISO 27001 increases a company's attractiveness as a business partner. By being able to **demonstrate the high level of information security**, they will grow their business opportunities. Large manufacturers will be more willing to favour their offerings over that of non-compliant suppliers. This compliance turns into a competitive advantage when entering new markets and long term supply arrangements.

Large manufacturers are constantly looking for suppliers in all fields and countries, as technology is rapidly advancing. Only relying on one suppliers for a particular part can become the tripping stone for a major brand. Similar examples exist in the crisis surrounding _airbag and brake manufacturers_ of foreign automotive manufacturers. Such crisis can lead to low level of trust in the eye of authorities and customers.

The manufacturing industry is used to having to comply with many regulations imposed by many countries, which cause additional costs just because of some requirement based on an outdated ideology in the minds of the political establishment.

By using ISO 27001 efficiently they can also become **better equipped to meet regulatory requirements**. In the USA every different state has differing laws in regards to sales, information security and taxation which affect manufacturers and their dealership networks. In Europe similar national peculiarities can cause additional complexity headaches even though the European Union has implemented standard regulations such as GDPR.

The investment in ISO 27001 helps them prove to the relevant authorities that they are taking the necessary steps to **protect sensible data**. Therefore, they are complying with laws and regulations.

Let me summarize what ISO 27001 does for you:

- Helps manage risks and improve security
- Establishes companies as trusted partners
- Compliance increases competitive advantages
- Meet legal and regulatory requirements

Large manufacturers benefit from ISO 27001 as it allows them to build a reliable and trusted supply chain. Governments are increasingly expecting social media, ITC related companies and education facilitators to implement ISO 9001 and ISO 27001.

The benefit of working towards this certification is, that the security level of the organization will be further strengthened.

Since information security requires not only technical and organizational measures to **ensure proper implementation**, one needs to also consider the human impact on security. Humans need time to adapt to change and turn the new ways of work into a natural habit. After the first introduction of an ISMS organizations will typically experience some levels of resistance. Building awareness and gaining honest commitment to a new standard takes time.

The ISO 27001 Standard sets high expectations. This leads to an implementation of sophisticated security controls (e.g., continuous monitoring, vulnerability management, penetration testing, etc.).

After completing the audit, the organization will **receive a detailed report**. Due to the intensity of the audit, more insights will be gained though the auditors feedback. The greater range of assessment will be a greater strain on the organization as they are expected to demonstrate a **higher level of compliance** with the ISO 27001 Standard.

The external audits (a.k.a. certification audit) need to be conducted by **independent auditors**. They are <u>trained and certified</u> in the Standard. These audits are quite detailed and **impartial** in order to help organizations improve their security. Thereby, they will be better at protecting sensitive data and systems. By applying the ISO 27001 Framework, organizations gain access to its tools and guidance. This way, they can implement an effective ISMS.

3 The true nature of ISO 27001

ISO 27001 is designed as a scalable and flexible framework adaptable to all types of organizations. This allows **small and large companies** to implement ISO 27001 in a fashion that matches their individual characteristics.

After the audit has been completed, the auditor **submits the report** to the certification body. Once this documentation has been approved by the certification body, the certificate is published in its' verification database which can be queried using the certificate code. In order to be audited, your company needs to apply to a certification body for an ISO 27001 certification. An audit firm (e.g. BSI, DNV, SGS, TÜV Nord, TÜV Süd, Zurich Engineering) would be acting as the certification body. In contrast, a component manufacturer could be providing their ISMS documentation to its critical enterprise client. This is because some **large manufacturers often assess their suppliers** with their own audit teams. In that case they are acting in both roles, since at some point they will be assessed, too.

IAF is the International Accreditation Forum, which unites all national accreditation bodies. In order to maintain a global standard, IAF works with its members to find a common understanding how to assess organisations in accordance with a given Standard. The accreditation bodies (e.g., ANAB, DAkkS, UKAS) **survey and regulate** the activities of appointed certification bodies. Each national accreditation body monitors the quality of certification processes as well as the audit results.

The certification bodies appoint auditors and dispatch them to the to be certified organisations. Auditors **can only be appointed** by the certification body, after they have been <u>well introduced</u> into the audit process via a **trainee period and monitoring session**. In order for accreditation bodies to be able to enforce transparent governance, they set rules that help prevent fake certificates being used in any business transaction where they are a vital criteria for doing business together.

The control function is protected by a **contract structure** in which accreditation bodies hold contracts with the <u>audit providers</u>. This ensures that the results correspond to the desired objectivity and quality. The **rights and duties** of all participants – small or large – are respected.

3.1   ISO 27001 Standard Requirements

According to the ISO 27001 Standard, organizations are expected to implement a comprehensive information security management system (ISMS). The ISMS needs to contain all aspects of <u>cyber security, risk management, incident management</u>, and <u>access control</u>. In regards to risk management, organizations should maintain a risk management process that ensures **regular evaluation** of its cyber security, as well as **identification and management** of <u>risks</u> in a rapidly changing world. By implementing a process for incident management, organizations are able to respond to threats in a more resilient way. They gain the ability to **detect and respond to incidents**. <u>Business continuity</u> is highly dependent on their ability to restore operations after an incident.

Compliant organizations should enforce a level of data protection, which requires them to **implement security controls** to protect personal data (e.g., customer data, employee data) from **unauthorized access, manipulation and misuse**. The effective implementation of technical and organizational measures is a valid requirement of ISO 27001. These measures are designed to ensure **confidentiality, integrity and availability** of the data. This expands towards meeting the requirements of data protection laws (e.g., BDSG) and related regulations (e.g., GDPR).

Hence, the key items are:
- Risk management
- Incident management
- Protection of data privacy

In order to be ISO 27001 certified, an organization must implement the standard's requirements. Auditors will inspect the ISMS documentation and a variety of records, in order to evaluate the true level of compliance of an organization.

3.2 The ISO 27001 certification process

During the ISO 27001 audit the dispatched auditors will follow a comprehensive and systematic approach. Auditors will follow a structured process whereby they evaluate, if **the documentation reflects true adoption** of the standard or represents a faked compliance. Most professional organizations will have the financial and organizational resources to take ISO 27001 seriously.

The benefit of such an audit is a range of key learnings, which will **help improve an organization's information security**. Hence, preparing for the audit must consist of management commitment and gaining support from the entire workforce. This support will need to go beyond company borders as some suppliers (e.g., Recruiting agents, outsourced data centres, freight services) may have a critical influence in the success of an ongoing ISO 27001 Compliance.

These key items need to be achieved before the preparation phase is completed:

- Understand the standard's requirements
- Understand the scope of the audit
- Plan the ISMS implementation

These key items need to be achieved before the **implementation phase** is completed:

- Write all relevant ISMS documents
- Develop policies, procedures and processes
- Gather all relevant operational information
- Evaluate potential weaknesses and resolve them
- Train staff (incl. awareness trainings)
- Communicate to staff the next phase

These steps take place during the **audit phase**:

- Request certification audit from certification body
- Evaluation of key documentation (ISMS)
- Review of policies, procedures and processes
- On-site audits to gather evidence of effective implementation
- Resolution of identified deficiencies
- Adapting security measures to resolve issues

- Prove of corrective resolution of weaknesses
- Implementation of recommended improvements

These steps take place during the **certification phase**:

- The auditor provides a report and relevant evidence of the assessed level of compliance to the certification body.
- The certification body reviews the submitted documents and the auditor's recommendation for certification
- The certification body approves certification and issues the ISO 27001 certificate

3.2.1 Who conducts ISO 27001 audits?

Only **accredited certification bodies** may conduct audits upon which a certificate is issued. This audit conclusion document highlights the compliance of the organisation's information security management system in regards to the Standard.

Following organisations are <u>examples</u> of accredited certification bodies:

- France: SGS

- Germany: TÜV Süd, TÜV Nord, DEKRA

- United Kingdom: BSI, INSPEC, …

- USA: ISA, AEA, DLS, Schellman, ISOQAR

- Netherlands: Mazars, SISCERT, FACTOCERT, CERTVALUE

You can find a regional list of certification bodies on this website:

https://acato.de/iso-27001-zertifizierungsstellen/

Hence, organizations will receive recognition for their outstanding initiatives to ensure a level of information security.

3.2.2 Types of ISO 27001 Audits

Based on the chosen standard and the organisation's risk profile, a certification body will have to develop a basic set of parameters to establish the needed audit resources.

Companies in the manufacturing have equipment that could lead to accidents, injury or environmental pollution. These organizations display a **high risk**. If their products can cause accidents, injury or environmental pollution, then they also add a certain level of risk to the general risk rating. Certification bodies need to take this into consideration.

In contrast, companies with no life threatening risks to employees and customers, will have a **lower risk pattern**. Certification bodies could come to the conclusion, that an audit will not need to be so lengthy as in a manufacturing business.

Both examples apply to potentially dangerous situations in ISO 9001 (Quality Management) and ISO 27001 (Information Security) business environments. As you have learned in previous sections, information security includes **all digital data** (e.g., in databases) and **physical data** (e.g., in paper files). When confidential information gets in the wrong hands, it can also become a life threatening risk.

ISO 19011:2018 offers these types of audits:
- Onsite Audit
- Remote Audit

On-Site Audit

On many situations certification bodies will dispatch to a client's site an auditor or audit team. Depending on the **volume of audit work**, one needs a certain number of auditors onsite which are directed by a lead auditor. This a regular approach for any ISO standard (e.g. ISO 9001, ISO 14001, etc.).

As previously mentioned, every organization has its own risk profile which influences the **number of audit days** and the complexity of sampling. This is also a key aspect when considering mixing an onsite with remote audit.

All audits consist of stage 1 and stage 2. During **stage 1**, the lead auditor will be **reviewing the ISMS documentation** the client submitted. Based on his findings he will develop a checklist, that will guide him and his co-auditors through stage 2. Stage 1 is usually done without auditee interaction. Depending on the auditors contractual relationship (employee or freelancer) with the certification body, the auditor will review the documentation in his office at the certification body office or in his own premisses (not belonging to the certification body.

As we move towards **stage 2**, the lead auditor will arrange an appointment with the auditee and will **provide a preliminary list** of documents his audit team will want to inspect in the auditee's premises. Companies with a medium to high risk should usually **not be audited remotely**, unless it is a small satellite unit of the company without justifiable need for auditors travelling long distances (e.g. 12h flights) just to conduct a 2 hour interview. Such short interviews can be easily conducted via video conference tools (e.g. Zoom, MS Teams, Google Meets, Webex).

Organizations just starting to implement an Information Security Management system (ISMS) are well advised to start with a system audit before moving to a certification audit. This system audit focuses the core requirements of the Standard.

This will also require inspection of:
- implementation of a security policy,
- risk management process,
- incident management process and
- the access controls

After this audit one will receive a report identifying all areas of non-compliance. This document will also **state recommendations** for improvement. Only after resolving all identified issues and making use of the recommendations, one should consider embarking on the next route towards an ISO 27001 certification audit. It is absolutely **not necessary nor required** to conduct a system audit, in order to be eligible for an ISO 27001 certification audit. Be careful: Some consultants are **overselling** "*system audits*" (or "*system certificates*") as if they were ISO 27001 certification audits. A "*System Compliance Certificate*" is not an official ISO 27001 certification certificate!

Online / Remote Audit

The second type of audit is called "Remote Audit" and is only suitable for organizations with a low risk profile. The stage 2 of a certification audit can be conducted via remote audit, when an onsite audit **offers little benefit**.

A best example are SaaS Companies whose team is organized as completely remote. Often Startups of different sizes can have their key people working from home, while being separated from each other several flight hours.

It makes little sense for an auditor to travel to every key person's home being <u>more hours in an aeroplane</u> or at an airport <u>than actually spending for the audit work itself</u>.

This is why some certificate bodies utilize auditors based far away from the clients for remote audits. There is no advantage of hiring a local auditor as the auditee is so spread apart that the certification body's offices will always be out of reach (max. 3 hours car drive). This is a great example for a digital business with no manufacturing or direct risk to life and health of people.

Of course, there are <u>startups and large companies</u> that develop products which can become **very dangerous** for humans, animals and nature. In such cases, the dangerous parts of a business should be audited on sight. We can reasonably presume a startup is not developing rockers or aircraft engines in the engineer's backyard.

In a later section of this book you will gain deeper understanding in the regulatory aspects that allow or govern a **remote audit**.

3.2.3 Typical Misunderstandings & Scams

One must be careful with the terms *"information security"* and *"cyber security"*, as they are often used in the wrong context. <u>Cyber security</u> is a **subsection of information security**. information security protects digital (*e.g. files*) and physical assets (*e.g., paper records*).

Another misconception is that you **buy a template** and don't need to add any additional information. Unfortunately, this typically will lead to the <u>ISMS failing to pass stage 1</u> of the certification audit.

ISO 27001 Certificate Scams

Sometimes companies think that you can buy an ISO 9001 or ISO 27001 certificate. They typically lack the understanding, that they need to develop their own management system documentation, before the auditor can evaluate its conformity. You simply **can't buy a certificate**. Nevertheless, there are people out there selling fake certificates without any audit or documentation.

ISO 27001 Documentation Scams

Recently, I was astonished to find that a company had paid 12.000 EUR for a **16 page ISMS document**, while believing they would be receiving a certificate from an accredited certification body.

A tools manufacturer bought a certificate for 2.500 USD from an **Indian consulting company** selling fake ISO 27001 certificates. The company got a set of standard documents and a visit from a consultant, who simply inserted the company name and logo on site. Then left for lunch and returned to audit these previously edited documentation. Once the manufacturer's large client came to perform a supplier audit, this story emerged and the manufacturer realized he had been scammed.

An SME got sold an ISMS package for 9.500 GBP in return for a customized documentation and a system audit. The **system certificate** was promoted to the recipient, as if it were a certificate from an accredited certification body.

4 Getting ready for ISO 27001

In order to succeed with implementation and assessment, organizations need to prepare well. The documentation needs to match the requirements of ISO 27001. Too often templates purchased from the web are incomplete or even outdated. This is similar to what you can run into when hoping for a shortcut to ISO 9001 certification.

It is best practice to write a project plan and have a checklist at hand, so that one doesn't miss important items. Some organizations conduct an internal **GAP analysis** and then request an external advisor to run a second GAP analysis, when all documentation is completed and every person in the organization is actually using the new way of working with sensitive information.

4.1 Gap Analysis

In order to know how far developed the organization is before implementation of a compliant ISMS, one should assess the current situation. This is where a GAP analysis provides a realistic picture of the **existing security** and <u>what still needs to improve</u>. This way, the project team can prioritize the key issues to work on. By using the ISO 27001 framework as a guide towards an information security management system (ISMS), the organization will be able to not only comply with ISO 27001 but also adjust its ISMS to fit the organization's **unique business model**.

In many cases security will have been implemented as a technical feature in the IT Department. There might be some kind of documentation on how Active Directory, Firewalls, VPN and other IT Technology has been configured to match the current opinion on how to implement IT security. Unfortunately, information security is a large topic which includes many other items such as IT security or cyber security.

If there is some kind of documentation then this will help formulate the policies in the ISMS. Hence, a GAP Analysis will look at security policies, procedures and controls. These need to be compared to the requirements of ISO 27001. This eventually feeds into the to do list or checklist for building a compliant ISMS.

In order to ensure a realistic data collection, one will need to **speak to a variety of key people** (e.g., IT admins, CSO, IT Directors, Network Admins, Developers, Engineers, etc.) in the organization. Besides communication with technical staff, one needs to also communicate with **sales, marketing, logistics, facility management, procurement, HR** and other departments and locations.

Identifying **risks and vulnerabilities** helps establish a better understanding of the organizations current risk exposure. One can't expect in an organization that every employee knows what an ISMS is or how it relates to their individual work place. Hence, a first part of the communication during GAP analysis is to build awareness what information security actually means for the employee and the organization as a whole.

4.1.1 Why should we conduct a Gap Analysis?

Such a Gap Analysis will provide you with an informed assessment of:

- Degree of compliance gap of documentation for ISO 27001
- Level of scope matching with our documentation
- internal resources sufficiently aligned with IEC/ISO27001
- Realistic timeline to be ready for the audit

Based above analysis objectives we should work on answering the following questions, which I would like to explain to you here step by step:

How far are we from reaching compliance with ISO 27001?

The more documents or security policies are missing or incomplete, the lower the chances of satisfying the certification requirements. It is important to know what is incomplete or missing. It may be that at some time one was of the opinion this item is not relevant for the company's ISMS. If it is still not relevant, then one is well advised to add this information about why it is not relevant to a FAQ file. This is necessary if the item is on the verge of being questioned by the auditors.

Is the intended scope matching our documentation?

Furthermore, you need to evaluate if your selected scope matches your company and the documents you have prepared. Maybe you wrote too much or too little. An auditor might spot an **inconsistency** between your **chosen scope** and the submitted documents. If you are getting your first certification and your organization has complex areas, then you might be better off, to **limit the scope** to IT and other core activities.

This gives you time to expand the scope at a later time, without knocking your heads into a way. This also is a good way to reduce your workload and stress level if you are currently very busy with other business matters. The only other alternative would be to outsource part of the complex documentation work.

Are our recourses sufficiently aligned with ISO 27001?

Keep in mind that recourses are not only capital, equipment and time but also people. You need to train your employees **according to the risks** they are having to handle. A person handling credit card data is juggling a higher information risk than the marketing assistant.

Everyone needs to understand what ISO27001 means for their personal work environment. If your team is not sold on the need to become ISO 27001 compliant, then you could experience a negative interview experience, should the auditor sense a lack of commitment from the organisation.

What will be a realistic timeline to achieve certification readiness?

Based on above mentioned aspects, you need to be realistic in regards to **how long you will need to fix** missing documents, inconsistencies, incomplete trainings or mindset conflicts. **Bottlenecks** can be training backlogs due to high workload in relevant departments. If there is a need for IT forensic investigations or penetration tests, then outside experts might not be available at short notice.

4.1.2 How is a Gap Analysis conducted?

A comparison of documents and activities in regards to ISO 27001 requirements will be conducted based on:

- Interview with relevant staff
- processes and procedures

- Initiatives currently on the go

Secondly, a review of key documents in regards to data privacy, security policies and procedures will be necessary. This also includes an inspection of key processes and systems to make sure operational activities are in line with the ISMS and the standard.

After the assessment of the data, one needs to analyse hoe it compares to the requirements of ISO 27001:2022. Based on these insights, an expert should write a Gap Analysis Report.

The report should contain following valuable insights:

- Maturity of information security arrangements
- Specific gaps identified and what they mean
- Suggestions for adapting the scope to match the ISMS or to match in a more realistic manner the organizations available resources.
- A basic plan of how to fix these problems. This will also include the level of required human efforts to get mack on track.
- For a better understanding one uses a visual representation: the compliance status is summarized in a few core items marked with colours (red, yellow, green).
- Security control can be listed to better understand where the gaps exist and how severe they may be

How much time does a gap analysis require?

Depending on the complexity of the ISMS documentation, an expert might need 1-8 weeks to gain a realistic opinion of the situation. The documents of an SME can usually be reviewed within 2-5 days.

Some organizations like to use a Gap Analysis to make sure they are ready. This is not a requirement for certification. Usually this is necessary if you have not had any help from outside experts while writing the ISO27001 documentation.

4.2 Compliance roadmap

As part of every ISMS related project, an organization needs to first develop a project plan. This is an advisable step that doesn't need to consume a lot of work time but can **avoid costly gaps** in a growing project. Whether you are building an ISMS in accordance with ISO 27001 you will realize, that this is often like walking through a jungle. You gradually detect issues you were not previously aware off. You might even notice that you overlooked a requirement, because there is so much to be done.

Most people who are writing an ISMS an employee - of a to be certified organization - are doing this for the first time in their life. This is also a learning opportunity this person.

Follow these 4 steps:

- Identify gaps
- Rank identified gaps
- Select order of urgency
- Fix the gaps

Focus your time and energy on the most critical areas. Get your ISMS to be compliant with ISO 27001 within a reasonable time frame. If you keep leaving the project collecting dust for weeks, you will waste more resources having to reevaluate your progress and the gaps.

Next will be to **define the goals and activities** which need to be part of each step in your compliance road map. Look at your **security policies**: develop them and document them according to ISO 27001. Are your procedures well defined and written so that any reasonable person understands how to proceed?

Look at your technical controls: What do you have currently in place? Read the documentation created by your technical staff. Write your own <u>clean and standardized document</u> for each technical control. In order to not forget any vital items, use sharable sheets (e.g. google sheets or SharePoint). **Mind maps** also help to drill down in order to find forgotten items. Check with your technical staff to find out any <u>new or outdated item being left out</u> on the list.

A with every roadmap, you should **set mile stones**. By assigning dates to each waypoint you will be able to **track bottlenecks and efficiency**. Management will most likely want a simple *bi-weekly report on your current progress*. Keep it simple by using a visible flow diagram, which you can <u>update within a **few** minutes</u>.

You can also **list the required resources** (e.g., budget, people, tools, documents) and departments (e.g., Network Admins, Accounting, HR Trainers) below every step. Be careful <u>not to overload</u> your visual roadmap. As your project progresses, you will find the need to **add outside expertise** (e.g., consulting) and **technology** (e.g., DMZ, VPN, new phones). Without the adequate budget you will be misled to seek the cheapest outside resource, that will only help you for a limited amount of time or threats.

Once you have a clear picture of what needs to be done in which order and have **considered any critical dependencies**, then you can reach out to a greater amount of people to get feedback on the new compliance road map.

As with every business, there are times in the year when migrating critical systems, upgrading manufacturing facilities or introducing a new ISMS can cause severe problems in the operational flow of the business. Hence, check not only with stakeholders about the goals you set and the roadmap but also **gain their advice on dates**, that can cause severe operational disruption.

This way you reduce the stress on the organization during your introduction of the new ISMS into the productive side of the business. Collect the feedback and evaluate their concerns or challenges. Adapt your time plan to avoid bottlenecks and distress.

4.2.1 ISO 27001 implementation team

The ISO 27001 implementation team should consist of following team members

- Security expert (knows the ISO 27001 Standard)
- Business expert (knows business processes and requirements)
- Representatives from key departments (e.g., sales, legal, HR)

These people will be needed to **assist in the implementation** of the processes. Thereby you will gain approval and activate the necessary processes **with less resistance**. Eventually you will achieve that business goals align with the ISMS. By assigning clear roles and responsibilities to each team member, you avoid conflicts and unnecessary duplication of tasks. That is how to complete the project in time and without excessive budget overstrain.

As you prepare to roll out the new ISMS you will need to find ways to communicate with the relevant departments and the subject matter experts in your organization. ISO 27001 expects **top management to commit** to the ISMS and the accompanied way of handling information. Commitment not only includes **providing resources such as budget and people** but also to participate in the mandatory management reviews.

4.2.2 Identifying needed tools and technologies

An ISMS needs to be actively used in order to be effective. A collection of documents being forgotten on your file server will not help satisfy the requirements of the standard.

Identify the most needed tools and technologies to improve the security level. This can include a new firewall (e.g. Firewall as a Service – FaaS), a "Security Information and Event Management" (SIEM) tool or "Mobile Device Management" platform (MDM) or "Intrusion Detection and Prevention System" (IDPS).

As you select the tools, you will need to make sure, they actually **satisfy the requirements** of ISO 27001 and that of your business. The reporting and monitoring requirements are not available for all solutions on the market. As some staff will **need specialized training,** non-critical staff should be provided easy to understand awareness trainings. Picking the right training platform and courseware can take quite some time.

Tools, platforms and training are part of an effective security management. This is how to achieve your information security goals.

4.2.3 Identifying needed knowledge

In order to successfully implement an ISMS in your organization, you will need to educate your employees on what information security really means and why it matters to everybody's future. Those who are directly involved with **writing and defining policies** need to understand how ISO 27001 expects information security to be implemented.

This is why someone busy implementing information security in their organization will benefit from attending an implementation training. It is not enough to know the ISO 27001 standard as the **employees need guidance** on <u>how to conduct their daily tasks</u> according to the international standard. This is why, implementers need to **design information cards and hangouts** so that staff understand how maintain compliance.

Overcomplicating procedure manuals leads to **confusion and resistance**. This explains the reason for so many ISO 27001 projects becoming a nightmare for so many corporate employees, as lack of communication generates frustration for everybody.

5 Implementing ISO 27001 in your company

After knowing what has to be done and having assembled your project team, you will need to transition from preparation to implementation. There are many policies and procedures to be written.

The 4 phases of implementation:

- Develop and implement your policies and procedures
- Implement technical controls
- Implement organizational measures
- Ensure monitoring and continuous improvement

5.1 Develop and implement your policies and procedures

Establish the needed policies and procedures. Make sure they meet the standard's requirements. You will end up with a variety of security policies (e.g., incident response policies). While selecting and writing those policies make them **relevant, practical and effective** for your organization. Get support from your stakeholders by involving them in the draft and final version of each document group.

After writing the policies, you need to get them to become part of business life. Establish them and include methods to **enforce** them. Consider ways not only to implement but also to **monitor** them.

As an ISMS is used, you will need to **regularly review** the documentation, **update the content** and make every affected person aware of the implemented changes. Over the years, ISO 27001 has been updated and gained new or refined requirements. In order to remain compliant, one needs to **update the ISMS** to reflect the current standard and address issues known in the current security environment.

5.2 Implement technical controls

Technical controls are an important part of implementation. The protection of information needs a **human and technical response** to threat scenarios. Hence, technology must be configured adequately to reflect the desired **settings**. In order to make sure that your controls and settings are adequate, you will need to **test** them.

The best approach is to run vulnerability assessments and penetration tests. This helps to record all weaknesses and fix them before they become a severe problem to the organization. As previously mentioned, controls have to be regularly evaluated and updated. There are a variety of tools and services to help you benchmark your security infrastructure. Make use of **automation** where possible. **Simplify** your monitoring and reporting on the state of your ISO 27001 compliance.

Besides using tools, you need also to have people trained. Otherwise they are unable to properly set and use those tools defending your environment. Develop your training plan to reflect the mandatory tools for effective security implementation. As highly skilled staff is a **scarce resource** in today's world, companies need to **identify individuals** they can further develop to become new experts in important areas of the organization.

Therefore, effective technical controls need to be in place, so to be compliant with ISO 27001.

5.3   Implement organizational measures

The 3rd part of implementation is to establish organizational measures. These enable the organization to help protect information systems.

Organizational measures should include:

- security awareness and training programs

- incident response procedures

- develop a risk management framework

Every employee must be aware of their **security responsibilities**. The common understanding, that the organization is taking all necessary precautions to be ready for the event of a security incident, is important for the organizational mindset.

The standards like ISO 27001 expect you to have a **training plan** in place. In order to be more effective, you need to have several plans according to the different areas of your business.

Hence, the IT department needs much more technical training so to properly manage all the security technology, which is at their disposal. In contrast, an accountant or marketing manager is not going to configure the SIEM.

They need to have a **proper understanding of the threats** and how to make a security minded approach in their daily work. There are so many simple steps a non-technical user can take when receiving a potentially dangerous email.

Hence, non-technical staff needs their **customized security awareness program**. A marketing person is going to be many more hours connected with the internet than an accountant busy recording financial transactions inside the organization. This is why even administrative roles have **different risk exposures**.

We live today in a very connected world, so that even a foreman at the production line has access to emails, since he needs to effectively communicate with HR and Quality Control. This exposes even workplaces in factories to cyber threats. There is no one solution that fits all organizational roles.

If an incident does happen, we will need to make sure it is handled appropriately. Our **incident response procedures** need to be part of documentation. This information must be common knowledge and not hidden in a locker under trash.

Like with fire drills, you will need to conduct regular security exercises. There are a variety of tools from different vendors (e.g. Hornet Security in Germany) which help **test the resilience** of your staff. This way, people actually experience a simulated attack without being warned ahead. This way they behave like they would during a real attack. Afterwards you can explain to people what happened and how in future avoid being fooled by real attackers.

As last part of this section we need to take a look at our risk management, because it is an important component according to ISO 27001. Your **risk management framework** must be equipped to **identify, assess and remediate risks**. The objective of risk management should be to preserve the required confidentiality, integrity and availability of information as well as the information systems storing that data.

To ensure this objective is actually sustainable, one needs to conduct **regular risk assessments and update risk response plans**. The security tests help validate the capability of the organization to deal with the threats in a satisfying manner.

5.4 Ensure monitoring and continuous improvement

Having an ISMS in place is a great achievement, nevertheless, it needs to be active and in good health. To ensure its <u>effectiveness and relevance</u> to the organization's risk environment, you need to do following:

- Review and evaluate the effectiveness of policies, procedures and controls

- Make adaptations to address any identified weakness or vulnerability

In order to ensure alignment with ISO 27001 standard you should establish review cycles with these actions:

- annual security assessments

- periodic security audits

The sustainability of your ISMS and successful regular external compliance audits are dependent on **your efforts to monitor and improve your ISMS** <u>regularly</u>. Otherwise you will most likely experience a non-compliance with ISO 27001 with a few months or years. People start forgetting and **no longer care** about your policies, procedures and controls.

By <u>integrating monitoring and improvement</u> into your **routine security practices** you will have less effort to remain compliant as well as safe. <u>Plan regular meetings</u> in your *group calendar* so that you can review the current situation. The assessments need not only to be **reviewed** but should be **documented**. Keep in mind that people forget what was agreed on and that sometimes regular attendants might be absent to a meeting with very significant revelations.

Key topics for your review meetings:

- **Effectiveness** of security policies, procedures and controls

- Identified areas for **improvement**

- **Trends** in the threat environment

- Agreements on next measures to address threats (who, due date, resources needed, dependencies)

This way you can adapt your technical controls much faster to address the developments in the threat environment. You will realize, that your organization eventually becomes ahead of the pack. Instead of your organization being **disrupted and damaged** like the rest of the sector, you will have remained mostly unharmed.

Key benefits:

- Well **prepared** for potential incidents

- Competitive **advantages** due to output / operative stability

- Proactively **responding** to new risks

- Ability to **assess impact** of new vulnerabilities before they are used against the organization

- Updating **technical controls** and implementing controls with less strain

- ISMS is therefore **always up to date** and capable of providing an effective defence against dynamic threats

As you gain insights on ideal ways of **handling unforeseen events**, you will be able to adapt your **security awareness programs**. This way, you develop best practice guides matching your organization's characteristics.

6 Getting ready for the ISO 27001 audit

As you have succeeded in developing and implementing your ISMS in accordance with ISO 27001, you will soon want to get the ISO 27001 certification audit done.

You need to understand the scope of the upcoming audit. Prepare accordingly for the audit process and identify items that need special consideration. Look out for the issues many other companies run into.

If you are still unsure where you are, then ask for outside help.

6.1 Audit risks of a mature ISMS

Certification bodies look at the maturity of an ISMS in order to calculate the risk of the management system failing to ensure all governance policies are enforced. The less mature an ISMS is, the higher the risk of failure.

If an organization is already has a certified quality management system, then certification bodies assume a lower risk. You might now jump to the conclusion it might be good to first start a ISO 9001 project before applying to get your ISMS certified. Unfortunately, this maturity risk evaluation also applies to an uncertified QMS (or EMS …).

There are several factors that eventually contribute to a certification body's calculation of the needed audit days. Some companies think they can write an ISMS and then immediately have it certified. It does take time for people inside an organisation to understand and adopt the new ISMS as part of their work routine.

That is why some certification bodies assume an ISMS is mature after a **time period of 6 to 24 months**. The counter starts on the day, the ISMS is officially declared by management as active and to be embraced by all relevant business units, departments and people.

I prefer to describe this step as the **establishment phase**, because it sits right between an implementation phase and the certification phase. If auditors find an ISMS has not been properly implemented and adapted to business reality after activating the ISMS, then they will most likely rate it as non-compliant.

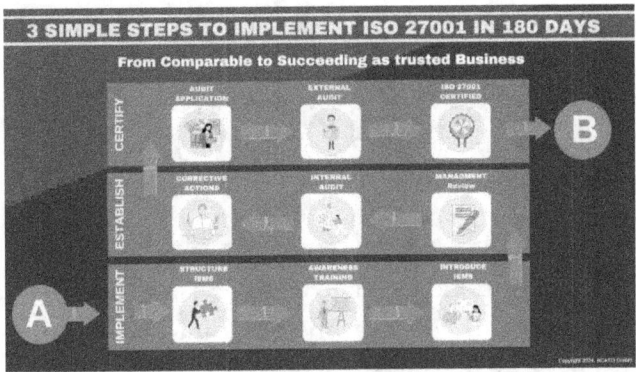

Above picture explains the process in a very simple way. During the establishment of the ISMS, it will be necessary to do an **internal audit** and a **management review**. Once these final steps are completed and necessary adjustments have been implemented, one can contact certification bodies to arrange an audit appointment.

6.2 Understand the ISO 27001 audit scope

An auditor will evaluate your information security management system against the requirements of ISO 27001. The audit will cover areas such as:

- Technical security measures

- Organizational security measures

- Policies and procedures

- Training programs

By knowing and understanding the audit's scope, you will be able to get all documents, systems but also every potentially involved person ready for the auditor's visit.

Dedicate enough time to review your documentation. Does it satisfy all ISO 27001 requirements? Have you researched inside special interest groups, if there are insights into what auditors are particularly checking this year? Each year accreditors tell certification bodies to pay attention to areas, they have found to be a **weakness of previous audits** (conducted by all the certification bodies they have accredited).

Auditors will look at your risk management and all associated records. There are no companies in the world, where there are no kind of incidents. Everywhere a digital device breaks, gets stolen or lost. The larger the organization the higher the potential chance there has been such an incident. People delete files by mistake, people click on spam links and get infected or hard drives get dropped. Anything can happen within a year.

Make use of the scope to spot weaknesses you might have overlooked. Get someone to look at the documents, <u>who has not been involved with your ISMS project</u>. Ask them for feedback and any random ideas coming to their mind. As silly or irrelevant they might seem at first, maybe the y help you get relevant ideas.

The **audit methodology** involves a combination of **document review**, <u>interviews with key stake holders</u> and onsite sampling as well as testing some of your security controls.

6.3 Prepare for the audit

While you are getting ready to submit your documentation and to receive the audit ream on site, you will need to complete some important items on your checklist:

- Collect all ISMS related documents
- Collect evidence to support effectiveness of ISMS
- Assemble your ISO 27001 audit support team

The ISO 27001 audit support team will usually be similar to your ISO 27001 project team. You need to expect auditors to call upon such people as they are **able to provide insights and evidence** about your organizations way of handling security topics.

Make sure to allocate sufficient resources for the entire ISO 27001 audit process. Have **sufficient staff** for the audit. Allocate sufficient budget for the expenses related to this certification project (e.g., travel cost, audit fees, software licencing, equipment, external advice).

In order to add **an extra layer of preparation**, you should get external security experts to <u>identify weaknesses</u> in the organizations defence. **Make the improvements** before submitting your documents to the certification body.

Your organization must <u>understand the requirements</u> of the standard. It is not a good idea to focus on paper and technology but to submit the certification request without having conducted the awareness trainings.

Do not let people in the organization ignore the upcoming audit. Ensure everyone understands, **why it is so critical for the company** to become ISO 27001 <u>compliant</u> and successfully <u>pass the audit</u>.

Update your project plan to reflect where you are and what steps still need to be completed. Don't key aspects slip away into the dark.

Make sure following **4 key aspects** are in line with the standards requirements:

- Evidence of compliance
- Technical Security Measures
- Organizational Measures
- Readiness Assessment

Auditors will look for evidence of compliance. If they have the feeling that evidence is fabricated or is barely existing, they might consider this to be an non-operational ISMS.

This is what they will look at in regards to evidence of compliance:
- security policies, procedures, controls
- evidence of measures

Technical Security Measures (a.k.a. TOM) will also be part of the assessment. You need to have technical security measures implemented so that staff know what is expected. Otherwise systems (IDPS, SIEM, Firewalls, Routers, Switches, Virtual Machines, etc.) will not be **properly configured**, so that even a non-technical person will quickly spot discrepancies (e.g. admin password being "password").

During the evaluation of existing Organizational Measures, auditors will want to find out, how well employees have been made aware of threats and expected behaviour. If the **staff you trained**, left your company months before the audit, then it is a bit of an inconvenience having to explain yourself: you **didn't hire** new qualified staff and didn't make an effort to **training remaining staff**?

You need to at least fill the gap temporarily by spreading the responsibilities across the existing team/department, until a new qualified candidate has been hired. Even hiring a freelancer for the time being, is better than failing the costly assessment and loosing contracts with major clients.

Finally, your Readiness Assessment will show the level or readiness your organization is in regards to the ISO 27001 standard. Resolve any vulnerabilities in time. Conduct penetration tests to further identify and eradicate weaknesses in your information security.

6.4 Typical challenges and pitfalls

You may encounter some of the following challenges:
- Lack of documentation
- Inadequate security measures
- Inadequate preparation

<u>Let me address each of the 3 mentioned types of challenges:</u>

A lack of documentation will cause auditors to **suspect inconsistency and lack of commitment**. This problem arises when either security measures have rudimentary description and guiding content in the core document or when the expected records are <u>not available</u>. It is understandable that not every technical system provides usable and exportable records.

Nevertheless, you can still **create your own record manually** and add screenshots (from firewall statistical graphics) into your word document. Inadequate security measures are related to **missing or inconsistent** configuration of systems. Many kinds of software (e.g., CRM, Backup, …) that provide access via user accounts usually offer an **assignable set of <u>roles and permissions</u>**. Check that every key item is properly implemented and configured.

Auditors will sense whether a person is insecure due to this being their first audit or whether they fear an inadequate preparation might lead the auditor to a **severe non-compliance discovery**. It is normal for every person who has never been at the receiving end of an audit, to be nervous and trying to have everything overly prepared. Hence, make an extra effort to invest time into reviewing all your items and having conversations with all the people, <u>who might be involved</u> during the auditor's visit. This will help you avoid an inadequate preparation and boost your emotional confidence.

7 How the ISO 27001 Audit will be conducted

In this chapter we will be taking a closer look at how to navigate the ISO 27001 **audit:**

- Understanding the audit process
- Understanding the role of the auditor
- Key aspects during audit
- Typical challenges and pitfalls

As with any kind of audit according to standards (e.g. ISO 27001:2022) an audit process will consist of several steps (preparation, ..., writing final report).

The auditor will ask several questions which you are supposed to be able to answer. No one expects you to know the answer to everything. Knowing who to call upon for help answering a certain question, is always a great way to include other people in the audit.

7.1 Understanding the audit process

An auditor will assess the policies, procedures and controls of an organization. Having to check a lot of documents and conducts interviews is **time consuming** for everyone. Auditors have a limited time to get everything done. By you understanding the audit process, you will reach your goals with **less haste and less stress**.

The audit phase consists of a set of objectives and outcomes. The auditor needs to **thoroughly check** the organization's information security management system. Keep in mind that it is expected and mandatory that the organization conducts a **self-audit (a.k.a. "Internal Audit")**, by which the organization proves it can identify any gaps or areas for improvements between external audits.

The external audit will usually start with a **documentation-based plausibility check** (ISO 27001: Stage I of the audit). The **comprehensive on-site audit** (ISO 27001: Stage II of the audit) will look at documentation referenced by the ISMS. This is also where interviews help the auditor evaluate, if the staff actually know, how to handle security in the expected manner.

Once the auditor has completed his investigation, the audit report will have to be **written and uploaded** to the certification body's audit coordination platform. An audit report will consist of <u>findings and recommendations</u>. The organization needs to use these insights to improve its security. Ignoring these issues and <u>not fixing them</u> could cause severe issues at the <u>next surveillance audit</u>.

Once the audit report has been accepted by the certification body's review team, the certificate will be issued to the organization. This is seen as a **3rd party validation**. The certificate can be checked online by any party that knows the certificate number or company name.

This published information serves as a <u>verified overview</u> of the current state of the organization's ISMS compliance.

7.1.1 Understanding the role of the auditor

Understanding the role of the auditor helps manage the expectations of both sides. Literature often refers to an auditor also as an "assessor". This person needs to be trained and certified in the ISO 27001 Standard.

There is a shortage in ISO 27001 auditors because of the deep knowledge and experience needed. That is why you need to expect a certification body or assessment provider to require plenty of time ahead, as they have limited resources. You might encounter an audit appointment in **6 or even 18 months**. Use the time to become more confident with using your ISMS.

The lead auditor is assigned an audit client and **arranges all scheduling** with the client directly. As soon as the key items are clarified, he will have to gather an audit team. If the certification body sets 4 or more audit days, then there will usually be 2 or more auditors involved. Having the required number of co-auditors is not easy. The larger the client the more audit work has to be processed.

Furthermore, the auditor must be **objective, impartial and free** of any **conflict of interest**. The last requirement further limits the amount of available auditors, because certification bodies are required to avoid sending an auditor to inspect an organization he currently has or recently had dealings with.

Hence, if a person left your organization 3 years ago in order to become an auditor, this person needs to highlight to the certification body, that he had previously worked for that company. If he is currently advising his former employer on how to get the documentation ready for ISO 27001, then he is not allowed to audit his former employer.

If it were not so, the audit would be at risk of losing its confidentiality, integrity and independence. During the auditor training skills like **communicating, handling findings and formulating recommendations** are important. Accept the auditors visit as a great opportunity to gain access to this persons extensive knowledge. Auditors can provide guidance in regards to best practice strategies for improvement of your organization.

7.1.2 Remote Audits

Remote audits are defined within ISO 19011:2018 in chapter 5.5.3 where it is described as an audit taking place in 2 separate locations (auditor's office vs. client site) at the same time.

This is also discussed in following regulatory documents:

- IAF MD 4:2018
- IAF MD 5:2019
- DIN/EN ISO/IEC 17021-1:2015-11
- ISO/IEC 17021-3:2017 (EN)
- ISO 9001 Audit Practices Group (see Guidance on remote audits)
- IAF IS12:2015
- DIN EN ISO 19011:2018-10
- IATF 16949:2016-10

Remote audits are described as being conducted by an auditor in a far distant location not being the auditee's own business location.

IAF MD 4:2018

In Chapters 4.1 / 4.2 we find that the requirements are clearly stated what is in General accepted. Nevertheless, Chapter 4.2.5 explains that the **calculation of audit time** and review needs to take additional aspects into consideration. Thereby, highlighting following remote audit ways as potentially acceptable:

- Telephone conference
- Internet based conferences
- Interactive web based communication
- Electronic remote access to the auditee's documentation and management processes

IAF MD 5:2019

The IAF document IAF MD 5:2019 helps deal with the complex calculation of required auditing time in relation to Quality Management (see: ISO 9001) and Environment Management Systems as well as Work Safety Management Systems (SGA-MS).

Previous releases of the standard **allowed a maximum of 30% remote** audit activity. With the release 2019 the limitations have been removed. Thereby allowing certification audits to be fully conducted as remote audits.

A few accreditation bodies are still refusing to allow more than 30% remote audit!

DIN/EN ISO/IEC 17021-1:2015-11

Conformity of locations where an audit may take place have some important disclosure requirements. In chapter 9.2.3.2 d of the standard document it is expected that the audit plan clearly discloses when and where an audit is being **conducted as a remote audit**. This is an important aspect as any 3rd party might presume that organization was fully audited by a team that was onsite.

ISO/IEC 17021-3:2017 (EN)

This standard release sets the **competence requirements** for staff involved in the audit and certification process. This is related to QMS audits. This is a add on to ISO/IEC 17021-1.

ISO 9001 Audit Practices Group

The guidance document on remote audits provides additional insights into the way of conducting remote audits. It also includes a risk related checklist for conducting remote audits.

7.1.2.1 Types of remote audit

As you might have gathered by now, remote audits are quite widely accepted in a variety of ISO standards. This was partly boosted by the pandemic years of 2020-2022.

Fully Remote Audit

Such a remote audit if only conducted remotely. No audit staff will visit the auditee's facilities or meet the auditee representatives for the audit at a common physical location. All communication takes place in a digital way.

Partly Remote Audit

Sometimes conducting a remote audit is helpful when visiting all auditee locations is not justifiable. Conducting a **part of an audit remotely** is often the best solution, when a distant satellite location of the auditee is only involved in the audit for a very short time. If an auditor would need more travel time, than what the actual review of documents and interview will take (e.g. 16 hours flight for a 1 hour conversation), then a remote audit is the best solution.

Remote Follow-up Audit

When an audit showed a small non-conformity then the organisation needs to fix and prove it was solved. In such a case a remote follow-up audit would still deliver the audit quality expected while avoiding unnecessary travel.

Expert Remote Audit

Some audits will need to have a subject matter expert, who is not fully available for the entire audit duration or is only needed for a very small portion of the audit work.

In such a case, it is nor reasonable to have the expert flown in at a high costs. Besides, the involved travel time might create a bottleneck as the expert might not have the space in the calendar to allow for such travel. It is absolutely sufficient then to make use of remote communication technology (e.g. Zoom, MS Teams, WebEx).

7.1.2.2 Opportunities and Risks involved with remote audits

Audit plans that include remote audits need to keep a backup plan, when a remote audit can't be conducted as expected.

Benefits of remote audit

One core benefit of using remote audit is that audit teams will avoid travels that cause CO_2 emissions as cars, aircraft and trains cause some level of pollution. The added flexibility of being able to schedule an appointment offers the chance to include interviewees who usually would not be available onsite. Furthermore, avoiding travel removes planning constraints and avoids unnecessary travel expenses.

Risks of remote audits

Nevertheless there are some risks you can't ignore. The technology used in the remote audit might fail or the people involved on behalf of the auditee are not skilled enough to use the technology. That can let an audit spiral out of the set time frame. Some audit sites have a limited bandwidth and WIFI connectivity on the auditee's premises. This can cause **loss of connection or misunderstandings** when spoken sentences have gaps.

Some auditors and certification bodies are <u>not comfortable</u> conducting the first certification audit with a new client as a remote audit. The auditee is unexperienced and may get confused due to the emotional element of the audit.

An additional issue is that of **confidentiality** and cyber security as a remote audit session might be hacked by criminals. Some auditee's dislike the thought of having people remotely accessing their networks. The topics of <u>data privacy</u> can also cause a remote audit to be cancelled, should any concern in relation to data privacy laws (GDPR) arise.

7.1.2.3 Remote audit competence & skills

A remote audit requires a skill set from both the audit team as well as the auditee's internal team:

- Communication
- Social communication competences
- Knowledge of Standard
- Remote audit skills
- Analytic skills
- Personal competences

7.1.2.4 Remote audit requirements

In order for a remote audit to be conducted in a reliable, trustworthy and competent way, there are a few key items to be expected a requirements:

- Internet connection with reliable bandwidth
- Availability of hardware needed for such remote conferences
- General agreement on how the remote audit will be conducted

- Securing of evidence of having conducted the audit remotely
- Avoidance or resolution of potential misunderstandings
- Auditor is the leading the conversations
- Experts may be joining the sessions when needed
- Auditor has sufficient knowledge about the organisation itself

The certification body will only be able to allow remote audits to be more than 30% if the respective accreditation body has allow edit.

7.1.2.5 Remote audit preparation

Getting ready for a remote audit is similar to conducting an onsite audit. Nevertheless, there are a few aspects I would like you to be prepared for.

These core items should be ready on both sides (auditor & auditee):

- Get your **technical equipment** (Microphone, Webcam, Speakers, Internet Connection, PC/Notebook/MacBook, LAN Connection, Conference System) ready.
- Get your selected room ready by **reserving it in time** and collecting **all the necessary tools** (Notepad, 3 different pens, ...). Make sure the lighting is sufficient. **Avoid any mess** in the background or in the room as it distracts both auditor and auditee.
- Make everyone in the audited **organisation aware of audit schedule** and the location of the video conference room.
- Gather all **ISMS related documents as digital files** and if necessary any printed document folders, so you can quickly get hold of the item you need during the audit interview
- If your organisation has a **dedicated IT person** for the equipment you will use, make sure you have their contact details and they are **aware of the importance of the audit**

event. They will be <u>ready to jump in to fix</u> any IT related problems. They are your cavalry. Treat them well.

Some auditors like to use 2 cameras and 2 monitors. Be aware that some auditors might just be using their notebook display or enjoy working on a 34″ curved monitor.

You might realize that working on an ISMS documentation can be very tiring. That is why I use a 34″ curved monitor with HDMI. Most Notebooks and MacBooks can be connected to such monitors. If you are using a Bluetooth keyboard and mouse, then remember to charge them up before the audit event. Beware that these nice monitors often do not have speakers integrated, which is no problem as you can use your notebook speakers. If you are using wired or Bluetooth headset, you will anyway have no audio issues (test before the audit date if you bought new equipment).

Should you only have a 15″-17″ Notebook display then do not worry. The auditor's screen will adjust and only show your screen in your display setting. If you use a desktop computer, then you will need to buy extra accessories. You can use Elgato FaceCam, Wave3 and their lighting equipment if you want to invest in really good accessories. They work well with Microsoft Windows 7 to 11.

Other auditors suggested also that you use 2 screens, if you don't have a large 34″ screen. Simply use one screen for the video communication and one for the documents you are currently discussing. In my opinion, set your workplace in the best way that really suites your personal preferences. Our suggestions are simply based on experience and our personal preferences.

7.1.2.6 Conducting the remote audit

As the audit takes place you will need to expect certain activities based on your company's industry sector and risk profile. If you are in a low risk service sector these would be the 3 items the auditor will look at:

- Management System Documentation
- Service processes
- Location of organisational Activity

When you are developing products an auditor will look these 3 core items:

- Management System Documentation
- Product Development and Support Service processes
- Location of development Activity

These items will be reviewed and discussed using Video Conference platforms such as *MS Teams, Zoom, Google Meets, Cisco WebEx*. Platforms such as *Skype, WhatsApp and Meta Messenger* are acceptable for quick notifications but not for discussing audit content.

In times of opensource and platform independent systems, companies might be using **Jitsi**, "**Big Blue Button**" or other tools. Make yourself familiar with the desktop and document sharing functionality of the chosen video conference system. Set up a test call beforehand with a team member to test using the different features.

7.1.2.7 Post Remote audit work

Once the audit has been completed, the auditor will have to write his audit report. Some people tend to record a video but this is not really an efficient way as one needs to listen again to the entire conversation. Hence, it is best to take notes the way you would do during an onsite audit

7.1.3 After the ISO 27001 Audit

After the auditor has finally left your company premises, you will surely breathe a sigh of relief. Make a <u>few notes</u> before going home. Your next workday will be to review your learnings and create your own preliminary to do list. The auditor might have already provided you an overview of the **nonconformities and observations**.

Start developing ideas, <u>how to productively resolve</u> the weaknesses and <u>utilize the recommendations</u> you received during the audit. You will need to develop corrective actions and find reliable ways to implement these necessary modifications.

Understand your results

Once you have been given a proper detailed summary on your current state of affairs, you will need to take time to **understand the <u>relevance</u> and the <u>cause</u> of the issue**. It is necessary, to understand the results of the audit, as otherwise you will waste energy and budget on an <u>inadequate response</u> to the nonconformities. You might even implement recommendations in the <u>wrong way</u> and thereby even <u>create for yourself new nonconformities</u>.

Where are you the best at?

As you work through the audit results, you will also realize that you are actually **good at some key areas**. Auditors look for the strong and the weak spots in an organization's security.

You might even have implemented procedures in a very good way so that you have developed for <u>your own organization a best practice</u>. Maybe you can use those insights to **develop a standardized best approach** at dealing with your weaknesses.

Area of nonconformities

There might be issues in your implementation of the ISO 27001 standard. The auditor will highlight these weaknesses as non-conformities. Look for recommendations on how to improve those weak spots. Some auditors provide a guidance with step by step description on how to fix these deficiencies. Be aware that some <u>accreditation and certification bodies</u> do not allow auditors to provide such detailed description of <u>how to fix your weaknesses</u>.

Risk assessment

If you receive a report with a risk assessment, then you can see how well protected you are. For each area you will receive marks or points or coloured grades. Use this to prioritize your activities to resolve all the weaknesses or inconsistencies.

Plan how to fix what is broken

Now that you have understood what is weak, broken or confused, plan how to fix these areas. Simply make a quick list of weaknesses and troublesome areas. Then work of expanding the detailed description of the problem and cause. Then elaborate on how you think you need to fix the item. Get feedback from subject matter experts in your organization and then get everybody to work on fixing the items. Once the auditor returns, he expects you to have done your homework!

7.2 Key aspects during assessment

Key aspects during assessment:
- Scope of the assessment
- Methodology of the auditor

By understanding the <u>Scope of the audit</u> you will know where to pay more attention to, as some systems will not be part of the evaluation. The scope helps the auditor and the organization be more focused while avoiding waste of resources.

The methodology of the auditor ensures that the audit is conducted in a consistent and objective way. This allows the auditor to communicate his **requests, questions, findings and comments** in a productive way. The auditor expects the organization to comply with his information requests within a reasonable time. He has to process a lot of information and documents. So many policies, procedures, controls and records will have to be evaluated within a limited time.

The **less resistance** the organization displays, the **more time** is available, to <u>gain insights</u> from the auditor's <u>extensive experience</u>.

7.3   Avoid typical challenges and pitfalls

Typical challenges and pitfalls can be summarized as following key problems:
- Incomplete or outdated documentation
- Lack of understanding of ISO 27001 requirements
- Inadequate preparation
- Inadequate technical controls
- Lack of continuous improvement
- Inconsistent Internal Audit Documentation
- Failure to identify and address opportunities

It will be of benefit to you to go through the following insights into, why they cause so many unnecessary problems for organizations wanting to gain the ISO 27001 certificate.

7.3.1   Incomplete or outdated documentation

When you started working on your ISMS documentation you were collecting lots of information and records. As you gradually develop your implementer writing skills, the amount of data **can easily hide irrelevant, outdated or inconsistent documents**.

Tip: If you invest some time with your key departments, you can find out what has changed. Update the documentation or remove outdated content.

Before the assessment, make sure documents are complete. Accidents can happen. Deleting paragraphs by mistake or forgetting to add content from a merged document can cause inconsistencies. Auditors have the advantage, that they have not been reading your material hundreds of times over the past 12+ months.

Tip: You become blind towards inconsistencies. Get <u>someone else</u> to <u>proofread your material</u>.

Don't forget to check the documents you are referring to in the ISMS. Maybe some system related records have been renamed, removed or lost.

7.3.2 Lack of understanding of ISO 27001 requirements

When starting a ISO 27001 project, you will at first research what is required to gain the ISO 27001 certification. Your material grows and you eventually can believe to know all what is necessary.

It is advisable to take a **ISO 27001 Implementer Training** so to be knowledgeable and avoid unpleasant surprises during the external assessment.

In the worst case, the organization will be downrated because it did not meet the requirements of the standard. You need to understand <u>how to translate</u> the requirements into **your own organizational context**. That is why simply buying some template off the internet is the best way to fail or burn a lot of budget on external consultants trying to fix the template's inconsistencies.

7.3.3 Inadequate preparation

Having the right staff and resources sounds so logical. Unfortunately, organizations often forget to inform all the different stakeholders and staff of the data when the audit will take place on-site. Having the required people being <u>unreachable during the audit</u> can cause unforeseen problems.

Also make sure the required people have cleared a large enough window in their schedule in case the auditor has to reschedule his days flow of interviews and document reviews.

7.3.4 Inadequate technical controls

If your technical controls are only on paper but not in the operational reality of people's daily work, then auditors will recognize inconsistencies. Your technical controls need to satisfy the requirements of the ISO 27001 standard.

Your company network, your core systems (e.g., Backup servers, SIEM), and applications (e.g., ERP, CRM, …) are **properly secured**. A dirty server room makes no good impression. Get your desks and office space cleaned, tidy and fix any broken equipment. Broken power wall sockets are a bad taste of, how serious you take work safety.

7.3.5 Lack of continuous improvement

As with any kind of standard related certification, you will soon find out, that you will be regularly audited over the next few years. With ISO 27001:2022 you are expected to **continuously update** your documentation and work on internal improvements.

If you do not bother to take care of your ISMS over the period of 12 months, **you can't realistically fix your cracks** within a weekend. The surveillance audit will lead the auditor to clearly identify, that you are not improving your organization, documentation and security.

You have to get a process set up that not only monitors your security but also reminds you of your **monthly activities**. You need to keep reviewing your policies, procedures, and controls. An active ISMS will see improvements and changes taking place over the period of 12 months.

As you see in following image, phase 1 needs to introduce an ISMS and improve it not only in phase 1 but also in all later phases. Even after successful certification of your ISMS you need to regularly look for areas to improve and implement these opportunities for improvement (OFI).

7.3.6 Inconsistent Internal Audit Documentation

The weakness of the internal audit documentation is a typical issue often identified by auditors during the certification audit. Either the **audit report is far too short** and doesn't support the organization desire to improve the ISMS or the internal audit lacks consistency. Here, you might see an audit plan with very little focus on important sections of the ISMS.

The **periodic audit program** (PAP) is often only planned for 1-2 years. Ideally it has the internal audits planned for the next 6 years.

Another weak spot within such **audit programs** is often to be found in the selected audit areas: The internal audits planed after the initial audit have **no clear focus** on particular sections of Annex A. Hence, *selecting all areas* of Chapter 4 to 10 and all areas of Annex A is a **total**

overkill. Also selecting 2 areas of the annex (e.g. A.7 & A.8) is also a bit to unfocused. Section A.8 is very long, so its smarter to select from A.5, A.6, A.7 and A.8 several areas (e.g. A.5.1, A.8.12, A.7.4, etc.).

The idea behind these expectations is that the internal audit has a **limited time available** to inspect the ISMS and the <u>effectiveness</u> of it in relation to the organizations actual behaviour.

Another problematic aspect within internal audits is highly disputed by internal auditors, consultants and certification bodies as well as accreditation bodies: The proof of the **internal auditor's competence**.

So often auditors get to see an internal audit report written by someone unknown to them. This where things get a little bit hot as the certification auditor **needs some form of evidence** supporting the competence of such internal auditor. As these internal audit report often do not come with some form of **training certificate**, the auditor has to ask the organization to <u>request a proof of competence</u> from the internal auditor. Such person is often part of a 3rd party (e.g. freelance consultant or management consultancy).

For most seasoned auditors delivering some form of training certificates is a **totally normal request**, without any kind mal intention. Whether the internal auditor is a freelancer or an employee at a very large consultancy, the certificate is usually reaching the client <u>within days</u>. Unfortunately, some people respond to such a request in a very weird way.

As many certification bodies often hire consultants to act as freelance certification auditors, these seasoned auditors often also take up assignments as internal auditors for their own consultancies or of cooperation partners. For these people it is a no brainer, that you need to repeatedly **gain new knowledge** by attending trainings and working on projects as well as <u>taking exams</u>. Before a freelancer may be appointed by a certification body, these certification auditor must prove their competence by **not only a CV** but <u>training certificates, certifications</u> and **provable experience**.

The **standard** demands from internal auditors a <u>certain level of competence</u> in order to conduct such an internal audit properly. It **doesn't prescribe** that such a person takes an **exam** or attends a physical **classroom training**.

Nevertheless, the accreditation bodies demand from certification bodies that their auditors <u>do not simply accept a vague claim of competence</u>. Hence, a **CV is not a satisfactory** proof of competence, expertise or other form ability to conduct such an internal audit.

7.3.7 Failure to identify and address opportunities

It's often observed that organizations struggle with addressing opportunities. The standard outlines how to manage both risks and opportunities. Frequently, companies use templates that don't address opportunities.

Certification audits increasingly focus on identifying and managing opportunities. It's crucial to define a methodology for managing opportunities, including creating an opportunity register. It's easy to immediately view opportunities from a risk-oriented perspective. Reading the few relevant documents, management might seem to avoid opportunities altogether, as the risks appear daunting. However, opportunities offer significant advantages for an organization.

The best approach is to consult the sales and marketing departments, as they inherently have a positive mindset. They see strong opportunities for revenue, growth, and new business.

8 Industry specific Advice

In this section I will prove you with some key advice for the Service, Education and Manufacturing Industry.

8.1 ISO 27001 in the Aviation Industry

The aviation industry consists of **aircraft manufacturers**, **airlines**, **maintenance** and **training** facilitators, **catering** and **fuelling** services. When it comes to processing data, we need to realize that the aviation industry has a wide range of data types and sources. On the one hand, the human resources area generates a lot of personal data from **training, recruiting, hiring** and performance related evaluations. This kind of data is highly sensitive as it is tied to a range of people.

On the other hand, the **booking systems** of airline process a lot of data as customers book flights, buy upgrades or gain frequent flyer status due to their **travel activities**. This data can not only used to generate a *behaviour profile* but also misused by criminals. This data is not only processed by the **airlines** but also by the **airport and security services**. Hence, cyber criminals can find a multitude of entry points in order to get hold of sensitive data.

Payment transactions will be a source for accessing credit card details which can be sold on the **dark web** to credit card fraudsters. As passengers provide their passport details, airline have to relay this sensitive data to the **security authorities** in a variety of countries. This exposes them (and all those involved in making this complex data exchange possible) to data theft risks which can be used by impersonators and fraudsters.

This <u>range of vulnerable entry points</u> makes it necessary for airlines and aircraft manufacturers to **require their direct suppliers** to add ISO27001 to their operational reality. Due to the mounting pressure on such suppliers, this is also being passed on to <u>their own suppliers and service providers</u>. Hence, a **recruiting agency** or a **flight school** or a **caterer** will have to become ISO 27001 certified.

8.2 ISO 27001 in the Education Industry

The education industry often has to handle a lot of information from students, pupils, employees or other people they are providing trainings to. This is why more and more <u>regulators expect</u> **private schools**, **academies**, **universities** and **training** facilitators to achieve ISO 27001 compliance. Protecting the data of training participants is a necessity due to data privacy laws and regulations.

With introduction of **NIS 2.0** the European union has recognized that the education sector is also an <u>important component</u> of the infrastructure. This lead to a terraced approach where an organization rated as essential, will effectively have to ensure its **<u>suppliers and subcontractors are also compliant</u>** with the EU regulations. So, if you have a <u>training facility</u> or offer a learn management platform (**LMS**) based on the SaaS business model, then you will need to gain an ISO 27001 certificate in order to remain competitive in your niche.

8.3 ISO 27001 in the IT Industry

ISO 27001 is an ever growing factor for companies operating in the IT industry. Whether your company is IT Equipment manufacturer, an **internet design agency**, a **software development Service** or a **software manufacturer** – you will gradually be required to prove your reliability in regards to information security.

Software manufacturers and ecommerce software providers are constantly troubled by **source code vulnerabilities, hacking attacks and IP theft**. Due to an increasing need to speed up the development, companies are often having to higher outside programmers to help build components for their core products. As in ISO 9001 also ISO 27001 expects additional efforts to protect R&D efforts from compromise.

Internet providers and data centres have already adapted their operations by fully embracing ISO 27001. When it comes to **IT Service providers** and **managed service providers** we often see that those who have adopted ISO27001 have a greater chance to grow their business in a sustainable way.

A certificate is not a ticket to rapid growth as it requires you to take great care in protecting sensitive data. Although IT people often think ISO 27001 is a topic only assigned to the information technology experts, they underestimate the importance to attach responsibilities for its adoption to the executive management at the top level of the organization. Thereby, there is a greater chance to gain access to the necessary resources (budget, people, time, equipment and priority).

8.4 ISO27001 in the Manufacturing Industry

The Manufacturing Industry has a variety of standards it is used to having in place, such as quality management documentation based on ISO 9001. ISO27001 adds an additional level of business continuity and reliability to a manufacturer.

With the mounting cyber risks large clients are become more aware of the threats that may harm them by going piggyback with the unintended help of manufacturing companies they buy products from.

In the **automotive industry** car manufacturers are increasingly demanding that suppliers either get a **TISAX assessment** <u>or an ISO 27001 certificate</u>. Due to the lack of TISAX Assessors you will gain an audit appointment <u>faster by opting for the ISO27001</u> route. The basic concepts are similar. Keep in mind that TISAX will have greater technical detail in regards to, how you are ensuring that a hacker can't enter your data environment.

8.5   ISO 27001 in the Service Industry

The service industry has a wide range of fields where companies can contribute to our daily lives. When these organizations are processing sensitive data they may expose interested parties to undesirable risks. That is where ISO27001 will drive a wedge between <u>certified service providers</u> and those who just avoid the necessary effort to protect 3rd party information.

As the <u>automotive sector</u> accesses services from companies that are not producing automotive parts, the need for greater information security can't be ideally solved using the TISAX approach. This is why some car manufacturers and asking a range of small to large **service providers** (e.g., <u>internet marketing agencies</u>, merchandise design companies, <u>recruiting agencies</u>, printing companies) to set up an ISMS. Furthermore, they expect them to have it properly audited by an accredited certification body.

Consulting companies often are in contact with sensitive information owned or managed by their clients. Sometimes corporate clients make service companies sign an NDA. With the increased risks, an NDA <u>will not protect corporations</u> from long-term economy losses due to data breaches which occurred at smaller service contractors. This is why **management consultancies** are increasingly upgrading their information security posture by developing their own ISMS documentation before becoming ISO 27001 certified.

Marketing agencies are traditionally seen as handling design topics and textual content. In a digital world such agencies are no longer focused on offline marketing. Their talents are also driving revenues for their clients in the internet and on social media.

This is where consumers may be **submitting personal data** to <u>buy</u> products, <u>participate</u> in price draws or submit <u>inquiries</u> for test drives and other **sales related interaction**. This is an area where personal data can be at risk and <u>cause reputational damages</u> to corporate clients. This is why agencies are realizing they need to differentiate themselves from other carefree competitors, who neglect information security.

9 How to get the most out of this book

You can access a range of additional material I have created to supplement this book from my website. This material includes Checklists, short questionaries (use it for your own self-assessment), Introductory videos and previously recorded webinars. The supplementary content is in English and in German:

https://meetchrisbartsch.com/supplement-iso27001-book

Please keep in mind, that the content on the supplementary page will be regularly updated and expanded. Some of the checklists and short how to guides need time to be updated and created. These guides are often based on audit experience of certifications taking place in the EU and North America.

Newsletters & free Webinars

You can also sign up for the newsletter to stay up to date with new trends. Since webinars are often the easiest way to explain complex topics, subscribers will gain access to **live webinars** and recordings of previous information exchanges.

Training courses

There is an ISO 27001 implementer training course (see acato.de or **acato.co.uk**). Nevertheless, you will need to invest time into learning the details, should you want to write the ISMS documentation by yourself.

If you are considering to switch your career to become an auditor, then you can take the ISO 27001 Auditor course (see acato.de or **acato.co.uk**). That is self-paced video on demand training in English.

9.1 How to get help

This book is quite detailed in regards to strategy, tactics, implementation and equipment. You might have realized, that you are not necessarily stuck but need some sort of guidance.

A shortcut helps you save time and energy.

In the past I have advised clients from around the world. I eventually realized, what most business leaders lack in order to succeed in introducing information security based on standards like ISO 27001. Some people try to do it all by themselves but eventually procrastinate. Some people do not follow the route. Most people want to focus on their key activities as their time and HR capacities are limited. They would like to leave all the complex aspects of such ISMS projects to a trusted team.

At present we have a limited number of accounts we handle. Hence, we only take per month 5 new key accounts. If you and your company realize that you need guidance then we should have a conversation. Please be aware that we have set us a focus on particular industries and business types we see fit for working with us. This set criteria ensures that we do not take on clients we can't guide to success. It is absolutely critical, that the client is **capable and willing** to actively work on making success a reality.

You can contact our consulting teams at:
- info@acato.de or via +49 89 540 410 70
- info@acato.co.uk or via +44 1923 959 790

9.2 Autor's Profile

The author of this book grew up in multiple countries with a variety of business and manufacturing environments.

After secondary school in Germany, the author became an industrial business apprentice (Industriekaufmann) with **BMW** AG (Munich). During that time he got to see many different areas of the automotive business. This included a trainee assignment at Australia's largest BMW Dealership in Sidney, Australia. He assisted the head of the "electric, electronics and air conditioning" department. During this time he was involved in the documentation of the key electronic components in the core knowledge handbook (a.k.a. "Weißbuch") of the new BMW model (E46).

After studying informatics and participating in **Microsoft's** Training program, he worked at a former electronics subsidiary of **SIEMENS**. Then went on to develop software for eCommerce. He also worked as an Business Intelligence consultant for a Microsoft partner and was part of **KPMG's** Forensic Technology investigation unit.

Later on he founded his 3rd company: ACATO GmbH. Providing special forensics and disaster recovery services to a variety of corporations and government bodies. He has been providing his knowledge at several events for a variety of security services (e.g., **BKA** Mobilfunk Fachtagung, 2015), universities (**FH Aachen, 2016**) and industry congresses (IHK Sicherheitstage, Helpdesk forum, …).

Eventually he become an advising board member at a venture investment company in Amsterdam (NL), which used his forensic expertise to protect their investments in new fields of technology. Thereby becoming the president of the management board of their core services unit (Accounting, IT, Consulting & Legal) in Warsaw (Poland).

During this, he also contributed to developing **cyber security** and **ESG** related education programs for a new business education unit. Thereby developing a <u>new auditor training approach for ISO 27001</u>.

As a result, his German company expanded into empowering SMEs to improve their information security via consulting, education and audit services. Now companies across Europe get help in developing ISMS documentation and **cyber security strategies**.

He is also a certified **Lead Auditor** and part of audit teams at several certification bodies (**DNV, TÜV Nord, TÜV Süd**, etc.) in the ISO 27001 and ISO 9001 (IT industry) standard.

Christian has appeared multiple times on national **TV** in **Germany** (Pro7, n-TV) and **South Africa** (GauTV). Radio interviews included shows on BR2 and Deutsche Welle. He was part of 2 episodes of the **science programs** "Galileo" broadcasted on the European Channel TV Pro7. Furthermore, several articles were published indifferent magazines in Europe and the US.

During a conversation with *Apple co-founder* **Steve Wozniak** his ideas around training and continued education were confirmed by Steve.

You can find out more about the author and what his current focus is on by visiting his website at **meetchrisbartsch.com**

Or via LinkedIn: **www.linkedin.com/in/meet-christian-bartsch/**

9.3 Bibliography

Following literature assisted me in writing this book and therefore I am adding them here as references:

Reichheld, F. (2006), *"The Ultimate Question – Driving Good Profits and True Growth"*, Harvard Business Review Press, ISBN 978-1-59139-783-0

Brenner, M., Gentschen Felde, N., Hommel, W., et.al. (2022), "Praxisbuch ISO/IEC 27001", Hanser Verlag, 4th Edition, published 2022, ISBN 978-3-446-47395-9

Kersten, H., Reuter, J., Schröder, K.W., (2011), "IT Sicherheitsmanagement nach ISO 27001 und Grundschutz", Vieweg Teubner Verlag, 3rd Edition, published 2011, ISBN 978-3-8346-1599-6

Koubeker, A., et.al. (2015), "Praxisbuch ISO 9001:2015", Hanser Verlag, 1st Edition, published 2015, ISBN 978-3-446-44523-9

IAF Standard documents accessed: IAF MD 5:2019, IAF MD 4:2018, IAF IS12:2015, DIN/EN ISO/IEC 17021-1:2015-11, DIN EN ISO 19011:2018-10, IATF 16949:2016-10

ISO 9001 Audit practices Group (see Guidance on remote audits)

Weber, Stefan (2021), *"Nachhaltigkeit im Blick"*, Creditreform Magazin, Edition 12, published 12/2021 by Creditreform

9.4   Other Books by Christian Bartsch

The Sustainable Idea

The world of business is becoming even more complex. ESG is affecting companies business and funding activities.

This book explains how best make use of ESG while not drowning in endless cycles of creating paperwork.

ISBN: 979-8-8330-3548-1

Information Security based on TISAX Strategies

When you want to gain a preferred Level of TISAX Compliance, you need to build an ISMS that is adapted to your business and satisfies the automotive industry standard's requirements. This guide saves you and your team a lot of pain.

ISBN: 979-8-8650-6265-3